Joseph
Campbell

LOST GODDESSES OF EARLY GREECE

LOST GODDESSES
OF EARLY GREECE

A Collection of
Pre-Hellenic Mythology

Charlene Spretnak

Illustrated by Edidt Geever

MOON BOOKS

First Printing: March 1978

Book Design: Edidt Geever and Charlene Spretnak

Illustrations and Cover Design: Edidt Geever

Typesetter: Fremont Type; Fremont, California

Printer and Bindery: Lithocrafters; Ann Arbor, Michigan

Publisher: Moon Books
   P.O. Box 9223
   Berkeley, California 94709

   Moon Books is a women's publishing company committed to
   making a wide variety of feminist material available in the general
   market and to improving conditions for women authors.

Distributor: Women in Distribution (WIND)
   P.O. Box 8858
   Washington, D.C. 20003

   In addition to wholesale orders, single copies are available from
   WIND for the cover price plus 15% for postage and handling
   (overseas, 30%).

Library of Congress Cataloging in Publication Data

Spretnak, Charlene, 1946-
  Lost goddesses of early Greece.

  Bibliography: p.
  1. Goddesses, Greek. 2. Mythology, Greek.
I. Title.
BL782.S66 292'.2'11 78-1806

ISBN 0-931452-00-7
Manufactured in the U.S.A.
First Edition

*for our foremothers
from the beginning*

CONTENTS

To be gripped by the realization of deity in woman, the spring and harbor of life, mankind did not have to wait for the invention of agriculture. Everywhere, from Spain to Siberia, so many palaeolithic documents of this devotion have emerged, and with traits so specific recurring in neolithic relics, as to forbid the facile inference that this change, however epocal, in man's living habits could by itself account for what is loosely called "the cult of the Mother Goddess" . . . What evidence there is — and it is not a little — points to concerns more comprehensive and profound. This is the oldest godhead perceived by mankind.

— Gunther Zuntz
Persephone: Three Essays on Religion and Thought in Magna Graecia

There can be no doubt that in the very earliest ages of human history the magical force and wonder of the female was no less a marvel than the universe itself; and this gave to woman a prodigious power, which it has been one of the chief concerns of the masculine part of the population to break, control and employ to its own ends. It is, in fact, most remarkable how many primitive hunting races have the legend of a still more primitive age than their own, in which the women were the sole possessors of the magical art.

> — Joseph Campbell
> *The Masks of God:*
> *Primitive Mythology*

The whole of Neolithic Europe, to judge from surviving artifacts and myths, had a remarkably homogeneous system of religious ideas, based on worship of the many-titled Mother-goddess, who was also known in Syria and Libya. Ancient Europe had no gods. The Great Goddess was regarded as immortal, changeless, and omnipotent; and the concept of fatherhood had not been introduced into religious thought.

— Robert Graves
The Greek Myths

The habit of viewing Greek religion exclusively through the medium of Greek literature has brought with it an initial and fundamental error in method. For literature Homer is the beginning, though every scholar is aware that he is nowise primitive . . . . Homer presents, not a starting point, but a culmination, a complete achievement, with scarcely a hint of *origines* . . . . Beneath this splendid surface lies a stratum . . . at once more primitive and more permanent.

> — Jane Ellen Harrison
> *Prolegomena to the Study of Greek Religion*

INTRODUCTION

Gaia created the world, Pandora gave bountiful gifts, Artemis led her worshippers in ecstatic dances, Hera rewarded the girls who ran the first Olympic races, and Athena peacefully protected the home. These goddesses are among the earliest deities known in Greece, but the original mythology surrounding them has been lost. We know their names only through the relatively late myths of the classical period.

Yet for thousands of years before the classical myths took form and then were written down by Hesiod and Homer in the seventh century B.C., a rich oral tradition of mythmaking had existed. Strains of the earlier tradition are evident in the later myths, which reflect the cultural amalgamation of three waves of barbarian invaders: the Ionians, the Achaeans, and finally the Dorians. These invaders brought with them a patriarchal social order and their thunderbolt god, Zeus. What they found when they entered Greece was a firmly rooted religion of goddess worship. In various regions of the mainland and the islands a goddess was held sacred and was associated with order, wisdom, protection, and the life-giving processes (e.g., seasonal change, fertility of womb and field). Among the goddesses we know to have preceded the Olympian system are Gaia, Themis, Rhea, Pandora, Aphrodite, Artemis, Britomaris, Diktynna,

Selene, Hecate, Hera, Athena, Demeter, and Persephone.

However, these pre-Hellenic goddesses are themselves late, specialized versions of the Great Goddess, the supreme deity in most parts of the world for millenia. Her worship seems to have evolved from the awe experienced by our early ancestors as they regularly observed woman's body as the source of life. Paleolithic statues celebrate the mysteries of the female: woman's body bled painlessly in rhythm with the moon, her body miraculously *made people* and then provided food for the young by making milk. In a primitive culture, copulation is not usually associated with the miracle of new life; paternity was not recognized for a long while. A further mystery to our ancestors was woman's androgynous nature: she could draw from her body both women and men.

Perhaps the earliest Paleolithic statues uncovered by archaeology are expressions of the female body as living microcosm of the larger experiences of cyclic change, birth, renewal, and nurture. In time these energies became embodied in the sacred presence of the Great Goddess. Rituals in her honor took place in womb-like caves, often with vulva-like entrances and long, slippery corridors. As society evolved, so did the powers of the Goddess. She was revered as the source of life, death, and rebirth; as the giver of the arts, divine wisdom, and just law; and as the protector of peace and the nurturer of growth. She was all forces, active and passive, creative and destructive, fierce and gentle.

The Great Goddess was known by many names in many cultures. At various sites of her worship, certain attributes were stressed. Because the traits that were emphasized came to be associated with the local name for the Goddess, many derivative forms arose. The seeming multiplicity of deities is misleading since each was a facet of the one, omnipotent Goddess. Eventually, some of the derivative goddesses reproduced, always partheno-genetically in prepatriarchal mythology. If the child was a daughter, she joined her mother in admin-istering supernatural powers. If the child was a son, he became his mother's lover and held a sub-ordinate role in the mythology. In graphic repre-sentations the son/lover is always pictured as being smaller than the goddess and usually in the background. The original perception of the goddess as parthenogenetic source of life was preserved as sacred long after certain biological facts were recognized among her worshippers. The Virgin Mary reveals her strong connection to the ancient goddess tradition by giving birth parthenogenet-ically to her child.

In Greece the invaders' new gods, the Olympians, differ in many ways from the earlier goddesses. The pre-Hellenic goddesses are enmeshed with people's daily experiencing of the energy forces in life; Olympian gods are distant, removed, "up there." Unlike the flowing, protective love of a mother-goddess, the character of the Olympian gods is judgmental. Olympian gods are much more warlike than their predecessors and are often involved in strife. The pre-Hellenic goddesses are powerful and compassionate, yet those whom the Greeks incorporated into the new order were transformed severely. The great Hera was made into a disagreeable, jealous wife; Athena was made into a cold, masculine daughter; Aphrodite was made into a frivolous sexual creature; Artemis was made into the quite forgettable sister of Apollo; and Pandora was made into the troublesome, treacherous source of human woes. These prototypes later evolved into the wicked witch, the cruel step-mother, the passive princess, etc., of our fairy tales. Of all the great mother-goddesses, only Demeter survives intact; however, she is not included in the main group on Mount Olympus, in spite of the fact that she is a *very* old deity and was very well-known on both the islands and the mainland.

As Professor Jane Ellen Harrison pointed out many decades ago, most of the Greek myths are aetiological: the early ones arose to explain natural phenomena (e.g., seasons, dew) or primitive rituals (e.g., fertility, childbirth) and the later ones explain political and social changes in society. An example of the former is the story of Demeter bestowing the gift of agriculture. For millions of years, men and women had been hunting and gathering food, respectively. With the development of an assured, stationary source of food, life was altered radically. Since Demeter was regarded as the giver of crops, she was greatly revered throughout the Aegean. The cultivation of food, domestication of captive young animals, weaving of clothes, and making of pottery all fell within the domain of women and were the beginnings of the technology that has made the past ten thousand years such an abrupt departure from our earlier eras.

Another example of mythic explanation is the story of the rivalry between Athena and Poseidon. In a vote by all the citizens of Athens, the men voted for Poseidon and the women for Athena. Since the women outnumbered the men by one, Athena won. To appease the wrath of Poseidon, the men inflicted upon the women a triple punishment: they were to lose their vote; their children were no longer to be called by their mother's name; and they themselves were no longer to be called after their goddess, Athenians. Obviously, this myth mirrors a shift in the social organization of Athens.

Much information has been lost concerning pre-Hellenic religion. In order to reconstruct the myths, fragments must be assembled from various sources. One area of evidence is archaeological discoveries. Very early statues, shrines, picture-seals on rings, and labelled figures on ceramic vessels all point to the deeds and rituals associated with various goddesses. A second area is the writings from the classical period. Homer, Hesiod, Pausanius, Herodotus, Strabo, and others sometimes mentioned, and occasionally recorded rather fully, very old observances of goddess worship that had survived at certain sites in Greece. A third area is the oral tradition. Many of the stories were preserved among the rustic people, and at Ephesus in Anatolia the worship of Artemis was kept alive well into the Christian era; during childbirth the women insisted upon praying to Artemis.

It is true that the very ancient goddess religions are a chapter of women's "lost" history (some would prefer to say "stolen" and they would not be wrong), but they also comprise a larger field. We were all taught in school that Greek culture was the foundation of western civilization; these myths from the prehistoric era (i.e., pre-*recorded* history) represent the foundation of Greek culture itself. As for the exact delineation of this cultural foundation, our knowledge is incomplete. The latest edition of the voluminous *Cambridge Ancient History* deftly notes that various aspects of pre-Hellenic religion are "under lively discussion." Quite so. It is important that the evidence be aired, that connections be made, that particulars be debated. Yet the essence of these prehistoric myths will be grasped only if we can let go of a protective, supposedly detached pose and enter into the body of myths with true openness. If we can succeed in reading these spiritual stories with spiritual perceptions, a sense of continuity with our past may result.

The ten goddesses included in this book are those pre-Hellenic deities about whom enough information survived to reconstruct their stories in the original form (i.e., before the take-over by the Olympian system of mythology), although certainly no one could presume to reconstruct *exactly* a long-lost oral tradition. I take full responsibility for the manner in which these myths are written, but the elements and themes are not mine. They have been preserved by the most slender threads from our pre-recorded past. Every symbol, feat, or location associated with the various goddesses in the myths is based on firm evidence. Unfortunately, so much has been lost and so much time has passed, it is unlikely that we can ever recover the fullness of the ancient culture, even as archaeologists continue to uncover more clues. Perhaps the most striking feature that turned up again and again during the research is the pervasive unity of the mythmakers with nature. Their bodies are not separate from what goes on around them. They conceive of differing emanations of a goddess without contradiction. In their world there are no uncomfortable dissociations. There is only the Whole.

Charlene Spretnak
Berkeley, California
May 1977

AUTHOR'S NOTE

The seeds for this book were planted several years ago when I began reading of certain archaeological and anthropological discoveries. In the summer of 1975, I attended a weekend gathering on "Women and Mythology" conducted by Hallie Iglehart. She showed slides of ancient goddess statues and artifacts from the Mediterranean area and the Near East, and she talked about the numerous clues that indicate an earlier stratum of matrifocal mythology and culture preceded the patrifocal order we call "ancient civilization." I knew of the evidence from my reading, but Hallie's slides and artbooks brought the subject to life. The images stayed with me. The rest of the weekend was spent on explorations into our personal mythology, on recognizing recurring symbols and events, and on seeing in our lives the ancient mythic themes of transformation and rebirth.

The impetus for the book came some three months later when I was riding in our car with my daughter, Lissa Merkel. Her eye was caught by the logo of an oil corporation and she cried, "Look, Mama, a horse with wings!" She became very excited about the idea of a flying horse. I said, "Yes, his name is Pegasus and he's part of a myth. Myths are very, very old stories. Maybe we can find a book of myths in the library and I'll read them to you." Then I drove on farther and thought aloud,

". . . but the oldest ones have been changed." A trip to the public library confirmed what I suspected from the mythology weekend: there were no collections of myths other than engaging editions of Hesiod's and Homer's revisionist works. I went home and took my high school edition of Edith Hamilton's *Mythology* from the shelf. I leafed through it and read that "Zeus had punished men by giving them women"; that Pandora was "that dangerous thing, a woman"; and that from Pandora "comes the race of women, who are evil to men, with a nature to do evil." In the interest of mental health and a positive self-concept, this did not seem the best way to introduce an impressionable, four year old child to the riches of mythology.

Once I had decided to reclaim the pre-Hellenic myths from obscurity, I went straight to one of the best classics libraries in the country. To my surprise, I found that the large majority of classics scholars are interested only in mythology of the Homeric tradition and later. The indexes in their books may contain long lists of page numbers dealing with goddesses, but they almost always refer to the Olympian versions of the goddesses. The bulk of our current knowledge about pre-Hellenic goddess worship exists because of the work of only a handful of European classicists. Still, there were bits and pieces about the original nature of the goddesses to be gleaned from scores of other authors as well. (While researching the myths, I discovered that my daughter's name, Lissa, is derived from the Greek *Melissa*, a title for the priestesses of Demeter.) When my research was completed, the surviving fragments were pieced together and the myths slowly were composed.

Throughout this period, my most encouraging and unflagging supporter was my sister, Nikki Spretnak. I also wish to thank Professor Walter Burkert of the University of Zurich, who generously gave his time and advice on the manuscript while he was the Visiting Sather Professor of Classical Literature at the University of California, Berkeley. My illustrator, Edidt Geever, deserves special thanks for her long, hard hours on the drawings and for our easy collaboration on the design of the book. Finally I wish to acknowledge the loving support given during this project by my parents, Donna and Joseph Spretnak, and by many dear friends. I am especially grateful for the encouragement and detailed responses offered by Anne Kent Rush and Merlin Stone.

C. S.

GAIA

Gaia (also called Ge) is the ancient earth-mother who brought forth the world and the human race from "the gaping void, Chaos."[1] In the Greek imagination the earth is the abode of the dead, so the earth deity has power over the ghostly world. Because dreams, which often were felt to foreshadow the future, were believed to ascend from the netherworld, Gaia acquired an oracular function. One means of divination was incubation, in which the consultant slept in a holy shrine with her/his ear upon the ground. Another means was the pronouncements of a priestess, who spoke of the future while in a trance; she sat on a tripod over vapors arising from a crevice. Gaia's oracular function appears in records of her worship at Delphi, Athens, and Aegae.[2] She was the earliest possessor of the Delphic oracle, before Poseidon, Dionysos, or Apollo.[3]

In the Homeric *Hymn to Ge*, she is praised as "the oldest of divinities"; however, the poem is clearly rooted in the Olympian tradition because it addresses Gaia as "Mother of the gods" and "wife of starry Heaven." Long before she was regarded as mother of the powerful deities, she herself was the powerful deity. In time her son/lover, Ouranos, was added to her mythology.

Although eclipsed during the classical period by the Olympian gods, Gaia's impressive figure is always in the background. Greek citizens swore their public oaths to her.[4] The priestesses at the oracular shrine of Dodona preserved her name in their chanted litany: "Earth sends up fruits, so we praise Earth the Mother."[5] And at Delphi the priestess began her formal ritual address to the gods thus: "First in my prayer before all other gods, I call on Earth, primeval prophetess."[6]

THE MYTH OF GAIA

Free of birth or destruction, of time or space, of form or condition, is the Void. From the eternal Void, Gaia danced forth and rolled Herself into a spinning ball. She molded mountains along Her spine, valleys in the hollows of Her flesh. A rhythm of hills and stretching plains followed Her contours. From Her warm moisture She bore a flow of gentle rain that fed Her surface and brought life. Wriggling creatures spawned in tidal pools, while tiny green shoots pushed upward through Her pores. She filled oceans and ponds and set rivers flowing through deep furrows. Gaia watched Her plants and animals grow. In time She brought forth from Her womb six women and six men.

The mortals thrived but they were continually concerned with the future. At first Gaia felt this was an amusing eccentricity on their part. However, when She saw that their worry about the future nearly consumed some of Her children, She installed among them an oracle. In the hills at the place they called Delphi, Gaia sent up steaming vapors from Her netherworld. They wafted up from a cleft in the rocks, surrounding a priestess. Gaia instructed Her priestess in the ways of entering a trance and in the interpretation of messages that arose from the darkness of Her earth-womb. The mortals travelled long distances to consult the oracle: Will my child's birth be auspicious? Will our harvest be bountiful? Will the hunt yield enough game? Will my mother survive her illness? Gaia was so moved by their stream of anxieties that She sent forth other portents of the future at Athens and Aegae.

Unceasingly the Earth-Mother manifested gifts on Her surface and accepted the dead into Her body. In return She was revered by all mortals. Offerings to Gaia of honey and barley cake were left in a small hole in the earth before plants were gathered. Many of Her temples were built near deep chasms where yearly the mortals offered sweet cakes into Her womb. From within the darkness of Her secrets, Gaia received their gifts.

PANDORA

The *kore*, or maiden, form of the earth-goddess is Pandora. She is pictured on ancient vessels as a figure rising from the earth with outstretched arms. (This is the often-portrayed *anodos*, the arising of the goddess.) Sometimes she is labelled *Ge,* or *Anesidora* (she who sends up gifts), or *Pandora* (giver of all gifts).[7]

Classicists familiar with the original role of Pandora have called Hesiod's famous story, which features the goddess as a curious, troublesome girl, a "perverted version."[8] No longer does Pandora bring the abundance of the earth-goddess' gifts in her great jar (*pithos*), but only disease, misery, and death.

In addition to her deed, the nature of her birth also was altered by the Olympian system of mythology. Perhaps the most spirited exposé of this transformation was written by Professor Jane Ellen Harrison in 1903: "Pandora is in ritual and matriarchal theology the earth as Kore, but in the patriarchal mythology of Hesiod her great figure is strangely changed and minished. She is no longer Earth-born, but the creature, the handi-work of Olympian Zeus . . . . Hesiod loves the story of the Making of Pandora: he has shaped it to his own *bourgeois*, pessimistic ends; he tells it twice. Once in the *Theogony*, and here the new-born maiden has no name, she is just a 'beautiful evil,' a 'crafty snare' to mortals. But in the *Works and Days* he dares to name her and yet with infinite skill to wrest her glory into shame. Through all the magic of a poet, caught and en-chanted himself by the vision of a lovely woman, there gleams the ugly malice of theological animus. Zeus the Father will have no great Earth-goddess, Mother and Maid in one, in his man-fashioned Olympus, but her figure *is* from the beginning, so he re-makes it; woman, who was the in-spirer, becomes the temptress; she who made all things, gods and mor-tals alike, is become their plaything, their slave, dowered only with physi-cal beauty, and with a slave's tricks and blandishments. To Zeus, the arch-patriarchal *bourgeois*, the birth of the first woman is but a huge Olympian jest."[9]

THE MYTH OF PANDORA

Earth-Mother had given the mortals life. This puzzled them greatly. They would stare curiously at one another, then turn away to forage for food. Slowly they found that hunger has many forms.

One morning the humans followed an unusually plump bear cub to a hillside covered with bushes that hung heavy with red berries. They began to feast at once, hardly aware of the tremors beginning beneath their feet. As the quaking increased, a chasm gaped at the crest of the hill. From it arose Pandora with Her earthen *pithos*. The mortals were paralyzed with fear but the Goddess drew them into Her aura.

I am Pandora, Giver of All Gifts. She lifted the lid from the large jar. From it She took a

pomegranate, which became an apple, which became a lemon, which became a pear. *I bring you flowering trees that bear fruit, gnarled trees hung with olives and, this, the grapevine that will sustain you.* She reached into the jar for a handful of seeds and sprinkled them over the hillside. *I bring you plants for hunger and illness, for weaving and dyeing. Hidden beneath My surface you will find minerals, ore, and clay of endless form.* She took from the jar two flat stones. *Attend with care My plainest gift: I bring you flint.*

Then Pandora turned the jar on its side, inundating the hillside with Her flowing grace. The mortals were bathed in the changing colors of Her aura. *I bring you wonder, curiosity, memory. I bring you wisdom. I bring you justice with mercy. I bring you caring and communal bonds. I bring you courage, strength, endurance. I bring you loving kindness for all beings. I bring you the seeds of peace.*

THEMIS

Another of the earth-mother's emanations is Themis. Aeschylus portrays her as the oracular power of the earth deity and identifies her as "Themis and Gaia, one in form with many names."[10]

Themis is the force that binds people together. She is the collective conscience, the social imperative, the social order.[11] At first she is of the tribe; later in the *polis* she takes the shape of law.[12] Her name is believed to mean "steadfast," and she became the personification of justice and righteousness.[13]

In the Olympian system, Themis is allowed two functions, though "Homer has but dim consciousness of their significance."[14] She convenes and dissolves the agora on Mount Olympus. Zeus cannot summon his own assembly; he must "bid Themis call the gods to council."[15] She also presides over feasts. When Hera arrives, the gods rise up to greet her and hold out their cups in welcome; she takes the cup of Themis, who is first.[16]

THE MYTH OF THEMIS

When the first man entered a cave and witnessed the first woman's magic of drawing forth a new person from her body, Themis was there. *The young shall be fed and nurtured, protected and loved.* The humans increased in number, living together in small groups. They shared meat, nuts, plants, shelter, and the pleasure of their bodies. Themis was with them. *All who shared the bond of a woman's womb, you are her Family. You are indivisible.* The families multiplied, each woman giving birth within the aura of her mother's protection. Themis saw their needs. *All the families descended from one womb are a Clan. Stay together. Listen to the elders as I guide them.* Neighboring clans sought better water sources, needed new shelters, settled common ground. Themis united them in peace. *You who pass birth, love, and death on shared ground, who trade your skills and crops among your clans, you are a Village. Follow the judgments of your council as I guide them.* The villages spread into towns, sometimes cities. Themis watched and issued from Her oracles pronouncements of order, justice, and mercy. *Keep central your agora. There I will reveal the Law to your leaders. Swear your oaths in My name and they will stand until you are received into My earthwomb. Grow in righteousness. I will feed you.*

In this way, millennia passed and Greece prospered in her infancy. Innocence ended abruptly. Barbarian invaders swept down through her mainland and later her islands. They seized Themis at the outset. With the Goddess a bound captive, the invaders proclaimed the new order: children must be named after their fathers; cities must be fortified; power must be worshipped. They established their new god, Zeus, who ruled by the terror of his thunderbolt and procreated by deception and rape. Yet Themis would not be silenced. *You dare not crush the primal Order. When your new gods and your mutilations of our old Goddesses assemble on Mount Olympus, I alone will have the right to convoke them. I will not die.*

APHRODITE

Aphrodite is a fertility goddess, the primal mother of all on-going creation.[17] She is a virgin in the original sense (one-in-herself, not necessarily abstaining from sex but always remaining independent),[18] and has eternal beauty. Her sea birth is yet another version (along with that of Pandora and Persephone) of the *anodos*, the arising of the goddess.[19] Her ritual bath of renewal at Paphos is associated with that of Hera and Athena.[20]

In Crete the epithet *Antheia* (flower goddess) was connected with Aphrodite at Knossos. The title reveals an old link with herbal magic, and she is associated with the apple, myrtle, poppy, rose, and water-mint.[21] She is also maker of the morning dew.[22]

Aphrodite came into Greece through Cyprus and originally was from western Asia, where a young lover, Adonis, eventually was added to her mythology. The goddess was akin especially to Ishtar and Astarte.[23] In name, personality, and function she was unHellenic and, in contrast to

Athena, she was not really Hellenized by the time the Homeric poems were written. There she is "thoroughly anti-Achaean and treated with little respect."[24] Professor Harrison once again has strong words about the transformation of the goddess: "When Aphrodite is assimilated into the patriarchal Olympus, a foolish and futile attempt is made to fit her out with a husband: the craftsman, Hephaistos."[25] The net in which Homer represents Aphrodite as being caught by Hephaestus was, originally, her own as Goddess of the Sea, and her priestess seems to have worn it during the spring festival.[26]

Patriarchal tradition revised the story of the birth of Aphrodite to a rather extreme extent: this powerful, procreative goddess from Asia is portrayed as having been produced by the seafoam caused by the severed genitals of Ouranos, who had been castrated by his son, Cronos.

THE MYTH OF APHRODITE

Life was young and frail when Aphrodite arose with the breath of renewal. Born by gentle winds on the eastern sea, She alighted on the island of Cyprus. So graceful and alluring was the Goddess that the Seasons rushed to meet Her, imploring Her always to stay. Aphrodite smiled. Her stay would be never ending, Her work never complete. She crossed the pebbled beach and wandered over the hills and plains, seeking out all living creatures. Magically She touched them with desire and sent them off in joyous pairs.

She blessed the females' wombs, guarded them as they grew, and warded off love's pains at birth. Everywhere Aphrodite drew forth the hidden promise of life. Every day She kissed the earth with morning dew.

The wanderings of the Goddess carried Her far, yet each spring She returned with Her doves to Cyprus for Her sacred bath at Paphos. There She was attended by Her Graces: Flowering, Growth, Beauty, Joy, and Radiance. They crowned Her with myrtle and lay a path of rose petals at Her feet. Aphrodite walked into the sea, into the pulsing moon rhythms of the tide. When She emerged with Her spirit renewed, spring blossomed fully and all beings felt Her joy. Through seasons, years, eras, Aphrodite's mysteries remain inviolable, for She alone understands the love that begets life.

TRIAD OF THE MOON: ARTEMIS, SELENE, HECATE

Artemis is the goddess of untamed nature. Among the rustic people, she is the most popular goddess in Greece.[27] "Where has Artemis not danced?" is a Greek saying.[28] Central to her worship are ecstatic dances and the sacred bough,[29] most probably derived from worship of the ancient moon tree, source of immortality, secret knowledge, and inspiration.[30] Artemis assists females of all species in childbirth and gave the name *artemisia* to the medicinal herb now called mugwort, which is used to encourage delivery.[31]

Although Artemis was worshipped throughout Greece, she was especially venerated in Arcadia. There she dwelt apart in wild, untouched forests and was the most virginal of all the goddesses.[32] The other important site of her worship was at Ephesus in Anatolia, where her qualities of mother-goddess were emphasized. The Ephesians believed that a many-breasted image of Artemis fell from heaven.[33] (Eventually this phenomenon took the form of a breastplate garment on statuary.) Two early forms of this goddess were Britomaris of eastern Crete and Diktynna of western Crete.[34]

In Olympian mythology Artemis is made the sister of Apollo and the daughter of Zeus. Her mother is variously represented as Demeter or Persephone or, most commonly, Leto.[35] Her Arcadian nature as Lady of the Beasts is employed in her new role as patron of hunters. Early graphic representations of Artemis show her flanked by two lions; later she is shown standing on a lion; finally she stands with her bow, holding a slain deer in each hand. In the *Iliad* Homer gives Artemis "a feeble and even ridiculous part."[36]

Selene (also called Mene) is the moon goddess who pulls the full moon across the sky with her chariot. She usually drives oxen or steers, or sometimes horses. In her early forms, she herself is conceived of as a cow with the ancient "horns of consecration," which form a crescent moon. Selene is said to be "of great importance in magic,"[37] but little trace of her worship has survived.

Hecate is the goddess of the waning and dark moon. She has chthonic associations and rules over ghosts and demons. Ritually prescribed food, known as "Hecate's suppers," was offered to her as a form of purification, and her image was set before homes to avert evil.[38] She is adept at sorcery and is "the mother of witches."[39] At certain sites in Greece, Hecate's torches were carried around the freshly sown fields to promote their fertility.[40]

Olympian mythology portrays Hecate as the daughter of Hera and Zeus. In one of the patriarchal stories assigned to her, Hecate enrages her mother by stealing her rouge to give to Europa. Hecate flees to the earth and hides in the house of a woman who is in labor; her contact with this woman renders the goddess "impure."[41]

THE MYTH OF THE
TRIAD OF THE MOON:
ARTEMIS, SELENE, HECATE

When the moon appeared as a slender crescent, delicate and fine but firm in the promise of growth, Artemis roamed the untouched forests of Arcadia. The Goddess lived with Her nymphs amid the thick, wild growth where animals joined freely in Her games and dances. She loved new life. Whether at play or at rest, Artemis was ever alert for the rising moans of a mother giving birth. The wind brought to Her long, low sighs and staccato songs of pain expelled. If the mother was an animal, lying alone in a hidden cave or a sheltered pile of leaves, Artemis rushed deftly through the woods to her side. She brought leaves of Her wild artemisia for the animal to eat and spoke softly in the mother's own sounds. The Goddess gently stroked the bulging womb until the wet, squirming bodies emerged.

She fondled each one and placed them under Her protection: *Within these forests no harm will touch the children of Artemis.* If the mother was a human, the Goddess appeared instantly at her side bringing artemisia for a potent tea. She wiped the woman's brow and massaged her womb with delicacy and patience, even though She knew the result would be only a meager litter of one or sometimes two. Still, Artemis always appeared to a mother who called and always rejoiced with her at the moment of birth. The other mortals present would come forward for a look, asking, "How is the new one? Who is the new one?" Then Artemis would smile at the new One and whisper to the mother: *You may both enter My forests without fear and join Me on any night lit by the waxing moon.*

The joining began when the moon was new and continued each night with more and more of Her animals and humans coming to dance with Artemis. On the evening before the full moon Her sacred grove was filled with celebrants. They encircled a large tree that stood apart from the others, its smooth bark and leaves seeming silver in the moonlight. Artemis moved toward the tree and silence followed, but for Her doves cooing softly in the boughs overhead. The Goddess crouched as the Great She-Bear She once had been and touched the earth. From the roots, up the trunk, along the branches to the leaves She drew her hands. Again. And again. With each pass She brought forth new life: pale blossoms unfolding and falling away, tiny globes of fruit shining among the branches, and finally ripe, glowing fruit hanging heavily from the sacred boughs. Artemis gathered the fruit and fed Her animals, Her mortals, Her nymphs, and Herself. The dance began.

The animals were drawn to the tree. They rolled over its roots and encircled the trunk. In a larger ring the dancers raised their arms, turning slowly, and felt currents of energy rising from the earth through their legs, turning, through their trunks, turning faster, through their arms, turning, out their fingers, turning, turning, to their heads, whirling, racing, flying. Sparks of energy flew from their fingertips, lacing the air with

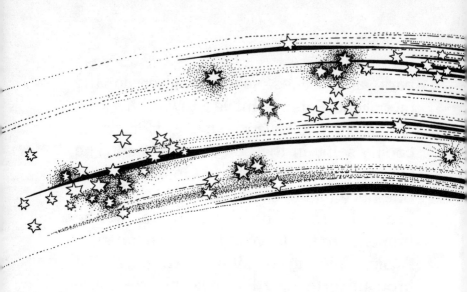

traces of clear blue light. They joined hands, joined arms, merged bodies into a circle of unbroken current that carried them effortlessly. Artemis appeared large before them standing straight against the tree, Her spine its trunk, Her arms its boughs. Her body pulsed with life, its rhythms echoed by the silvered tree, the animals at Her feet, the dancers, the grass, the plants, the grove. Every particle of the forest quivered with Her energy. Artemis the nurturer, protector, Goddess of the swelling moon. Artemis! She began to merge with the sacred tree, while the circle of dancers spun

around Her. They threw back their heads and saw the shimmering boughs rush by. When Artemis was one with the moon tree, the circle broke. Dancers went whirling through the grove, falling exhausted on the mossy forest floor.

Lying there on the earth, still breathing in rhythm with the earth, they stared up at the constant dancers in the heavens. Through the stars Selene was cutting a path with Her chariot. The winged Goddess drove a pair of oxen, whose horns echoed the crescent moon on Her own crown. Behind Her Selene pulled the full moon across the sky. She rose from the ocean and climbed steadily with the enormous disc to Her zenith, where it gradually shrank in size and She easily glided downward to the ocean once again. When Selene crossed the heavens, Her light flooded the earth, filtering down through the hidden cracks and crevices in the nature of mortal beings. They marked Her passage, joined in small groups to celebrate, and treated with awe those touched by Her magic.

But when the moon slipped away, shrinking gracefully into its own death, there were no festivities. The nights grew blacker and the mortals guarded themselves against visiting spirits from the underworld. Hoards of ghosts led by Hecate and Her baying hounds of hell roamed the earth on moonless nights. Yet She protected those mortals who purified themselves in Her name. With faces averted they offered Her ritual suppers at lonely crossroads, the gathering place of spirits. When Hecate's rites were observed, the black nights passed silently one into another. But if the Goddess was defied, She unleashed the power of Her wrath and swept over the earth, bringing storms and destruction. Animals howled in fright, while Her ghosts stalked freely.

Hecate's disturbances were fierce, yet not all of the mortals feared them. Some longed to join Her. In the dark of the moon small covens awaited Her near drooping willow trees. She appeared suddenly before them with Her torch and Her hounds. A nest of snakes writhed in Her hair, sometimes shedding, sometimes renewing. Until the new moon slit the sky, Hecate shared clues

to Her secrets. Those who believed understood. They saw that form was not fixed, watched human become animal become tree become human. They witnessed the power of Her favored herbs: black poppy, smilax, mandragora, aconite. Awesome were Her skills but always Hecate taught the same lesson: *Without death there is no life.*

HERA

Hera is essentially the goddess of women and fecundity.[42] Her connection with the three seasons of antiquity corresponds to the three stages of woman's life (maiden, fertile woman, old one).[43] In addition, she is connected to the three stages of the moon; such was the harmony with nature in earlier times that women's periodicity followed the moon's phases closely and their menstruation began at the new moon,[44] which was often summoned by their choruses.[45]

Hera was venerated at many sites in Greece, particularly on Crete and on Samos, but the chief center of her worship was at Argos. There several shrines were built to her, and she returned every year for a ritual bath in the spring Kanathos to renew her sense of virginity.[46] She also presided over "the sacred marriage," the merging of the lunar cow and the solar bull, which was a celebration of renewal and fertility in nature, especially that of the soil.[47] On Samos the sanctuary built for Hera was never exceeded in size by any temple in Greece.[48] The Samian women used *lygos* branches to stimulate menstruation and to aid in purification during their days of abstinence at the feast of the Thesmophoria[49] (see notes preceding the myth of Demeter and Persephone). (In order to present an inclusive portrait of Hera, the Argive and Samian forms of worship are combined in the following myth.)

At Olympia the goddess' Heraion long predates the temple of Zeus.[50] There races were run among the women "from time immemorial."[51] The runners were selected from three age groups, representing the three phases of the moon. "The well-founded view" among classicists is that the girls' races, which were held every four years at the feast of the Heraia, were far more ancient than the boys' races, which were first introduced only in the seventh century B.C.[52] When the men built a stadium at Olympia, an altar to Hera was included to commemorate her earlier reign. However, the only woman allowed to watch the contests was the priestess of Demeter Chamaine, the goddess linked with the soil, "probably because the competing men were later arrivals and had taken the ground for the stadium away from Demeter."[53]

In patriarchal mythology Hera becomes the wife of Zeus, although the connection of Zeus with Hera through the sacred marriage is a "late and superficial usage."[54] Hera is portrayed as Zeus' troublesome, disagreeable wife in a stormy marriage. The archaic theme of parthenogenesis is found in Homer's work several times in connection with Hera, linking her to the older matrifocal world.[55]

Professor Harrison summarizes the fate of the goddess: "Hera was indigenous and represents a matrilinear system; she reigned alone at Argos, at Samos; her temple at Olympia is distinct from and far earlier than that of Zeus. Her first husband, or rather consort, was Herakles. The conquering Northeners pass from Dodona to Thessaly. Zeus drops his real shadow-wife, Dione, at Dodona in passing from Thessaly to Olympia, and at Olympia, after the fashion of a conquering chieftain, marries Hera, a daughter of the land. In Olympos Hera seems merely the jealous and quarrelsome wife. In reality she reflects the turbulent native princess, coerced but never really subdued by an alien conqueror."[56]

THE MYTH OF HERA

On the morning of the new moon, the women of Argos left their homes and walked together to the Stream of the Freeing Water. They bathed and then gathered branches from the nearby lygos bushes, which they laid in a large circular bower. On this ring they sat throughout the day, each seated with the women of her mother's clan. With the blessing of the Goddess, the lygos encouraged the flow of their sacred blood that would complete the cleansing they had begun in the stream. Although the women fasted, their mood was not somber. They talked of their crops, their herds, their children and listened to stories told by the elders. As twilight approached, they began chants and songs that summoned Hera in Her manifestation of the new moon. When Hera appeared as a pale sliver climbing above the horizon, the women responded by lighting a fire in the center of their circle and continued the songs. Gradually Hera drew forth the blood of purification and renewed fertility. Gradually the chanting increased in tempo. Those who had received Hera's gift shared it with the young, the pregnant, and the old women by painting a red crescent moon on their foreheads. All rose, giving praise to the Goddess, and returned in a torchlit procession to their homes.

Hidden in the foothills nearby, the spring called *Kanathos* flowed secretly, silently from Earth's womb. Each year Hera appeared to the Argive women at the spring. She bathed in the cool water and emerged with Her virginity renewed once again — One-In-Herself, the Celestial Virgin. The women received the blessing of Hera's grace and crowned one another with wreaths of aster, blossoming with the Goddess' starflowers. They followed Hera to a broad terrace on the side of Mount Euboia, Her sacred ground.

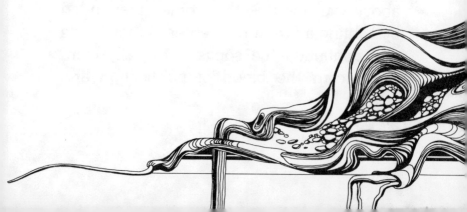

The Goddess looked down onto the plain stretching out before Her. All the people of Argos, all the animals, all the colors of spring had come together for the Sacred Marriage. Hera presided over the joining of the lunar cow and the solar bull. Then She looked out over the assembly and blessed the Argives with unfailing fecundity of field and womb. They celebrated the promise of their survival with dances and feasting. On that day began again the homage to Hera which continued throughout the year.

Every four years the benevolence of the Goddess was celebrated at the feast of the Heraia. At Olympia Hera watched the foot-races run in Her name. The races were run by girls divided into three age groups to represent the three phases of the moon and the corresponding three stages of woman's life. The winners were awarded an olive wreath and the honor of resembling the Goddess most closely. As Hera crowned the youngest winner, the girl addressed the crowd: *I am the new moon, swelling with magic, pure in my maidenhood, ever growing stronger.* The second winner spoke: *I* am the full moon, complete in my powers, making people with my rhythms, bathing them in light. The third said: *I am the waning moon, shrinking into peace, knowing all that went before, I am the old one.*

ATHENA

Athena (or Athene) was originally a Cretan goddess who watched over the home and town. Attributes of fertility and renewal are expressed in her association with tree (or pillar) and snake symbolism, respectively.[57] She is patron of wisdom, arts, and skills, and she especially protects architects, sculptors, potters, spinners, and weavers.[58] Athena was also the goddess of the matrifocal Pelasgoi of the Peloponnese;[59] in addition to her strong following on Crete, she was venerated at the following pre-Hellenic sites: Argos, Sparta, Troy, Smyrna, Epidaurus, Troezen, and Pheneus.[60]

When the Mycenaean princes of the mainland adopted and adapted Athena, she was assigned a martial character.[61] She became the shielded defender of their citadels, particularly Athens.

In Olympian mythology Athena is firmly established as the cold, rigid goddess of war. So suppressed and/or forgotten are her matrifocal Cretan origins that she is represented as a daughter born without a mother, having sprung fully armed from the head of Zeus.

THE MYTH OF ATHENA

In the Minoan days of Crete an unprecedented flowering of learning and the arts was cultivated by Athena. Dynamic architecture rose to four stories, pillared and finely detailed, yet always infused with the serenity of the Goddess. Patiently Her mortals charted the heavens, devised a calendar, kept written archives. In the palaces they painted striking frescoes of Her priestesses and sculpted Her owl and ever-renewing serpent in the shrine rooms. Goddess figures and their rituals were deftly engraved on seals and amulets. Graceful scenes were cast in relief for gold vessels and jewelry. Athena nurtured all the arts, but Her favorites were weaving and pottery.

Long before there were palaces, the Goddess had appeared to a group of women gathering plants in a field. She broke open the stems of blue-flowered flax and showed them how the threadlike fibers could be spun and then woven. The woof and warp danced in Her fingers until a length of cloth was born before them. She told them which plants and roots would color the cloth and then She led the mortals from the field to a pit of clay. There they watched Athena form a long serpent and coil it, much like the serpents coiled around Her arms. She formed a vessel and smoothed the sides, then deftly applied a paste made from another clay and water. When it was baked in a hollow in the earth, a spiral pattern emerged clearly. The image of circles that repeat and repeat yet move forward was kept by the women for centuries.

As the mortals moved forward, Athena guided the impulse of the arts. She knew they would never flourish in an air of strife, so She protected households from divisive forces and guarded towns against aggression. So invincible was the aura of Her protection that the Minoans lived in unfortified coastal towns. Their shipping trade prospered and they enjoyed a peace that spanned a thousand years. To Athena each family held the olive bough sacred, each worshipped Her in their home. Then quite suddenly the flowering of the Minoans was slashed. Northern bar-barians, more fierce than the Aegean Goddess had ever known, invaded the island and carried Athena away to Attica. There they made Her a soldier.

DEMETER AND PERSEPHONE

Demeter is the Grain-Mother, the giver of crops. Her origins are Cretan, and she has been strongly connected to Gaia[62] and to Isis.[63] Demeter's daughter, Persephone, or Kore, is the Grain-Maiden, who embodies the new crop. Every autumn the women of early Greece observed a three-day, agricultural fertility ritual, the Thesmophoria, in honor of Demeter. The three days were called the *Kathodos* and *Anodos* (Downgoing and Uprising), the *Nesteia* (Fasting), and the *Kalligeneia* (Fair-Born or Fair Birth).[64] The Thesmophoria, the Arrephoria, the Skirophoria, the Stenia, and the Haloa were rites practiced by women only and were of extremely early origin. They were preserved "in pristine purity down to late days and were left almost uncontaminated by Olympian usage"; they emerged later in the most widely influential of all Greek mysteries, the Eleusian Mysteries.[65] Isocrates wrote that Demeter brought to Attica "twofold gifts":

"crops" and the "Rite of Initiation"; "those who partake of the rite have fairer hopes concerning the end of life."[66]

The Homeric *Hymn to Demeter,* assigned to the seventh century B.C., is a story written to explain the Eleusian Mysteries, which honored Demeter.[67] The tale became famous as "The Rape of Persephone," who was carried off to the underworld and forced to become the bride of Hades. However, prior to the Olympian version of the myth at a rather late date, there was no mention of rape in the ancient cult of Demeter and her daughter, nor was there any rape in the two traditions antecedent to Demeter's mythology.

Archaeology has supported[68] what Diodorus wrote concerning the flow of Egyptian culture into Greece via Crete: "the whole mythology of Hades" was brought from Egypt into Greece and the mysteries of Isis are just like those of Demeter, "the names only being changed."[69] Isis was Queen of the Underworld, sister of Osiris, and passed freely to and from the netherworld. Demeter's other antecedent was Gaia,[70] the ancient earth-mother who had power over the underworld because the earth is the abode of the dead.[71] At certain sites in Greece, Demeter was worshipped as "Demeter Chthonia,"[72] and in Athens the dead were called *Demetreioi*, "Demeter's People"; not only did she bring all things to life, but when they died, she received them back into her bosom.[73] That the maiden form (Kore) of the goddess would share the functions of the mature form (Demeter), as giver of crops on the earth and ruler of the underworld, is a natural extension. The early Greeks often conceived of their goddesses in maiden and mature form simultaneously; later the maiden was called "daughter."[74]

In addition to the connections with Isis and Gaia, another theory holds that Persephone (also called Phese-phatta) was a very old goddess of the underworld indigenous to Attica, who was assimilated by the first wave of invaders from the north; the myth of the abduction is believed to be an artificial link that merged Persephone with Demeter's daughter, Kore.[75] Whatever the impulse behind por-traying Persephone as a rape victim, evidence indicates that this twist to the story was added after the societal shift from matrifocal to patrifocal, and that it was not part of the original mythology. In fact, it is likely that the story of the rape of the goddess is a historical reference to the invasion of the northern Zeus-worshippers, just as is the story of the stormy marriage of Hera, the native queen who will not yield to the conqueror Zeus. What follows is a pre-Hellenic version of the very ancient myth of the goddess who gave humankind the gift of agriculture and who ruled over the realm of the dead.

THE MYTH OF
DEMETER AND PERSEPHONE

There once was no winter. Leaves and vines, flowers and grass grew into fullness and faded into decay, then began again in unceasing rhythms.

Men joined with other men of their mother's clan and foraged in the evergreen woods for game. Women with their children or grandchildren toddling behind explored the thick growth of plants encircling their homes. They learned eventually which bore fruits that sated hunger, which bore leaves and roots that chased illness and pain, and which worked magic on the eye, mouth, and head.

The Goddess Demeter watched fondly as the mortals learned more and more about Her plants. Seeing that their lives were difficult and their food supply sporadic, She was moved to give them the gift of wheat. She showed them how to plant the seed, cultivate, and finally harvest the wheat and grind it. Always the mortals entrusted the essential process of planting food to the women, in the hope that their fecundity of womb might be transferred to the fields they touched.

Demeter had a fair-born Daughter, Persephone, who watched over the crops with Her Mother. Persephone was drawn especially to the new sprouts of wheat that pushed their way through the soil in Her favorite shade of tender green. She loved to walk among the young plants, beckoning them upward and stroking the weaker shoots.

Later, when the plants approached maturity, Persephone would leave their care to Her Mother and wander over the hills, gathering narcissus, hyacinth, and garlands of myrtle for Demeter's hair. Persephone Herself favored the bold red poppies that sprang up among the wheat. It was not unusual to see Demeter and Persephone decked with flowers dancing together through open fields and gently sloping valleys. When Demeter felt especially fine, tiny shoots of barley or oats would spring up in the footprints She left.

One day They were sitting on the slope of a

high hill looking out in many directions over Demeter's fields of grain. Persephone lay on Her back while Her Mother stroked Her long hair idly.

"Mother, sometimes in my wanderings I have met the spirits of the dead hovering around their earthly homes and sometimes the mortals, too, can see them in the dark of the moon by the light of their fires and torches."

"There are those spirits who drift about restlessly, but they mean no harm."

"I spoke to them, Mother. They seem confused and many do not even understand their own state. Is there no one in the netherworld who receives the newly dead?"

Demeter sighed and answered softly, "It is I who have domain over the underworld. From beneath the surface of the earth I draw forth the crops and the wild plants. And in pits beneath the surface of the earth I have instructed the mortals to store My seed from harvest until sowing, in order that contact with the spirts of My underworld will fertilize the seed. Yes, I know very well the realm of the dead, but My most important work is

105

here. I must feed the living."

Persephone rolled over and thought about the ghostly spirits She had seen, about their faces drawn with pain and bewilderment.

"The dead need us, Mother. I will go to them."

Demeter abruptly sat upright as a chill passed through Her and rustled the grass around Them. She was speechless for a moment, but then hurriedly began recounting all the pleasures they enjoyed in Their world of sunshine, warmth, and fragrant flowers. She told Her Daughter of the dark gloom of the underworld and begged Her to reconsider.

Persephone sat up and hugged Her Mother and rocked Her with silent tears. For a long while They held each other, radiating rainbow auras of love and protection. Yet Persephone's response was unchanged.

They stood and walked in silence down the slope toward the fields. Finally They stopped, surrounded by Demeter's grain, and shared weary smiles.

"Very well. You are loving and giving and

We cannot give only to Ourselves. I understand why You must go. Still, You are My Daughter and for every day that You remain in the underworld, I will mourn Your absence."

Persephone gathered three poppies and three sheaves of wheat. Then Demeter led Her to a long, deep chasm and produced a torch for Her to carry. She stood and watched Her Daughter go down farther and farther into the cleft in the earth.

In the crook of Her arm Persephone held Her Mother's grain close to Her breast, while Her other arm held the torch aloft. She was startled by the chill as She descended, but She was not afraid. Deeper and deeper into the darkness She continued, picking Her way slowly along the rocky path. For many hours She was surrounded only by silence. Gradually She became aware of a low moaning sound. It grew in intensity until She rounded a corner and entered an enormous cavern, where thousands of spirits of the dead milled about aimlessly, hugging themselves, shaking their heads, and moaning in despair.

Persephone moved through the forms to a large, flat rock and ascended. She produced a stand for Her torch, a vase for Demeter's grain, and a large shallow bowl piled with pomegranate seeds, the food of the dead. As She stood before them, Her aura increased in brightness and in warmth.

"I am Persephone and I have come to be your Queen. Each of you has left your earthly body and now resides in the realm of the dead. If you come to Me, I will initiate you into your new world."

She beckoned those nearest to step up onto the rock and enter Her aura. As each spirit crossed before Her, Persephone embraced the form and then stepped back and gazed into the eyes. She reached for a few of the pomegranate seeds, squeezing them between Her fingers. She painted the forehead with a broad swatch of the red juice and slowly pronounced:

> You have waxed into the fullness
>   of life
> And waned into darkness;
> May you be renewed in tranquility
>   and wisdom.

For months Persephone received and renewed the dead without ever resting or even growing weary. All the while Her Mother remained disconsolate. Demeter roamed the earth hoping to find Her Daughter emerging from one of the secret clefts. In Her sorrow She withdrew Her power from the crops, the trees, and plants. She forbade any new growth to blanket the earth. The mortals planted their seed, but the fields remained barren. Demeter was consumed with loneliness and finally settled on a bare hillside to gaze out at nothing from sunken eyes. For days and nights, weeks and months She sat waiting.

One morning a ring of purple crocus quietly pushed their way through the soil and surrounded Demeter. She looked with surprise at the new arrivals from below and thought what a shame it was that She was too weakened to feel rage at Her injunction being broken. Then She leaned forward and heard them whisper in the warm breeze: "Persephone returns! Persephone returns!"

Demeter leapt to Her feet and ran down the hill through the fields into the forests.

She waved Her arms and cried: "Persephone returns!" Everywhere Her energy was stirring, pushing, bursting forth into tender greenery and pale young petals. Animals shed old fur and rolled in the fresh, clean grass while birds sang out: "Persephone returns! Persephone returns!"

When Persephone ascended from a dark chasm, there was Demeter with a cape of white crocus for Her Daughter. They ran to each other and hugged and cried and laughed and hugged and danced and danced and danced. The mortals saw everywhere the miracles of Demeter's bliss and rejoiced in the new life of spring. Each winter they join Demeter in waiting through the bleak season of Her Daughter's absence. Each spring they are renewed by the signs of Persephone's return.

FOOTNOTES TO THE INTRODUCTORY NOTES PRECEDING EACH MYTH

1. H. J. Rose, *A Handbook of Greek Mythology*, New York: E. P. Dutton & Co., Inc., 1950, p. 19.
2. Lewis R. Farnell, *The Cults of the Greek States*, Vol. 3, Oxford: Oxford University Press, 1907, p. 8.
3. Jane Ellen Harrison, *Myths of Greece and Rome*, London: Ernest Benn Ltd., 1927, p. 68.
4. Farnell, p. 3.
5. Harrison, *Myths of Greece and Rome*, p. 68.
6. *Ibid.*
7. Jane Ellen Harrison, *Prolegomena to the Study of Greek Religion*, Cambridge: Cambridge University Press, 1922 (1903), pp. 280-281.
8. Farnell, p. 27.
9. Harrison, *Prolegomena to the Study of Greek Religion*, pp. 284-285.
10. Jane Ellen Harrison, *Themis: A Study of the Social Origins of Greek Religion,* Cambridge: Cambridge University Press, p. 480.
11. Harrison, *Themis*, pp. 485 and 533.
12. *Ibid.*, p. 484.
13. *The Oxford Classical Dictionary*, Second Edition, 1970, p. 1052.
14. Harrison, *Themis*, p. 482.
15. *Ibid.* (Homer, *Iliad*, XX.4-6)
16. *Ibid.*

17. E. O. James, *The Cult of the Mother Goddess: An Archaeological and Documentary Study*, New York: Frederick A. Praeger, Inc., 1959, p. 147.
18. Harrison, *Myths of Greece and Rome*, p. 26; also M. Esther Harding, *Women's Mysteries, Ancient and Modern,* London: Rider & Company, 1971 (1955), p. 103.
19. Harrison, *Prolegomena to the Study of Greek Religion*, p. 309.
20. *Ibid*, p. 311.
21. R. F. Willetts, *Cretan Cults and Festivals*, London: Routledge and Kegan Paul, 1962, p. 285.
22. *Ibid*.
23. James, p. 147.
24. *Ibid*.
25. Harrison, *Myths of Greece and Rome,* p. 26.
26. Robert Graves, *The Greek Myths*, Volume 1, Baltimore: Penguin Books, 1961 (1955), p. 71.
27. Martin P. Nilsson, *The Minoan-Mycenaean Religion*, New York: Biblo and Tannen, 1971, p. 503.
28. *Ibid*.
29. Martin P. Nilsson, *A History of Greek Religion*, Oxford: Oxford University Press, 1949, p. 28; also *Ibid.*, p. 503.
30. Harding, *Women's Mysteries, Ancient and Modern,* p. 46.
31. Harrison, *Myths of Greece and Rome*, p. 37.
32. *Ibid.*, p. 33.

33. James, p. 151.
34. Nilsson, *The Minoan-Mycenaean Religion,* pp. 510-511.
35. *New Larousse Encyclopedia of Mythology,* English Edition, London: Prometheus Press, The Hamlyn Publishing Group Ltd., 1968, p. 121.
36. *The Oxford Classical Dictionary,* p. 127.
37. Rose, p. 34.
38. Nilsson, *A History of Greek Religion,* pp. 204-205; also James, p. 153.
39. Robert Graves, *The White Goddess,* New York: Farrar, Straus, and Giroux, 1966, p. 200.
40. Harding, p. 129.
41. *New Larousse Encyclopedia of Mythology,* p. 165.
42. James, p. 144.
43. Harrison, *The Myths of Greece and Rome,* p. 19.
44. C. Kerenyi, *Zeus and Hera,* Princeton: Princeton University Press (Bollingen Series 65-5), 1975, p. 130.
45. *Ibid.,* p. 126.
46. Harrison, *Prolegomena to the Study of Greek Religion,* p. 311.
47. James, p. 144.
48. Kerenyi, p. 149.
49. *Ibid.,* p. 155.
50. Harrison, *Myths of Greece and Rome,* p. 18; also Kerenyi, pp. 133 and 135.
51. Kerenyi, p. 133.

52. *Ibid.*, p. 134.
53. *Ibid.*, p. 133.
54. Willetts, p. 111.
55. Kerenyi, p. 56.
56. Harrison, *Themis*, p. 491.
57. James, p. 146.
58. *New Larousse Encyclopedia of Mythology*, p. 107.
59. George Thomson, *The Prehistoric Aegean*, New York: The Citadel Press, 1965 (1949), p. 267.
60. Graves, *The Greek Myths*, Volume 1, p. 47.
61. James, p. 146; also Nilsson, *A History of Greek Religion*, pp. 26-27.
62. Farnell, pp. 28 and 48-50.
63. Harrison, *The Religion of Ancient Greece*, pp. 51-52.
64. Harrison, *Prolegomena to the Study of Greek Religion*, pp. 120-131; also Willetts, p. 152.
65. *Ibid.*, Harrison, p. 120.
66. Harrison, *The Religion of Ancient Greece*, p. 51.
67. James, p. 153.
68. Sir Arthur Evans, *The Earlier Religion of Greece in the Light of Cretan Discoveries*, London: Macmillan and Co., Ltd., 1931, p. 8.
69. Harrison, *The Religion of Ancient Greece*, p. 52.
70. Farnell, pp. 28 and 48-50.
71. *Ibid.*, p. 8.
72. *Ibid.*, pp. 48-50.

73. Harrison, *Myths of Greece and Rome*, p. 73.
74. Harrison, *Prolegomena to the Study of Greek Religion*, pp. 263 and 274.
75. Gunther Zuntz, *Persephone: Three Essays on Religion and Thought in Magna Graecia*, Oxford: Oxford University Press, 1971, pp. 75-77.

REFERENCES

Note: This is not a complete bibliography of all the books I consulted, but rather a listing of those that were most relevant to the pre-Hellenic goddesses. Many would also be useful to anyone wishing to rediscover the original nature of closeted goddesses in other cultures. — C.S.

J. J. Bachofen, *Myth, Religion, and Mother Right,* translated by Ralph Manheim, Princeton: Princeton University Press (Bollingen Series 84), 1967 (1854).

Robert Briffault, *The Mothers,* London: George Allen & Unwin Ltd., abridged edition, 1959 (1927).

Z. Budapest, *Selene: The Most Famous Bulleaper on Earth,* Oakland: Diana Press, 1976.

Joseph Campbell, *The Masks of God: Primitive Mythology,* New York: The Viking Press, 1959.

Judy Chicago, *Revelations of the Goddess,* to be published.

Elizabeth Gould Davis, *The First Sex,* Baltimore: Penguin Books, 1972 (1971).

Helen Diner, *Mothers and Amazons: The First Feminine History of Culture*, New York: Anchor Press/Doubleday & Co., 1973 (1929).

Sir Arthur Evans, *The Earlier Religion of Greece in the Light of Cretan Discoveries*, London: Macmillan and Co. Ltd., 1931.

Lewis R. Farnell, *The Cults of the Greek States*, Oxford: Oxford University Press, 1907.

Robert Graves, *The Greek Myths*, Baltimore: Penguin Books, 1961 (1955).
The White Goddess, New York: Farrar, Straus and Giroux, 1966 (1948).

M. Esther Harding, *Women's Mysteries, Ancient and Modern*, London: Rider & Company, 1971 (1955).

Jane Ellen Harrison, *Mythology*, New York: Harcourt, Brace & World/Harbinger Books, 1963 (1924).
Myths of Greece and Rome, London: Ernest Benn Ltd., 1927.
Prolegomena to the Study of Greek Religion, Cambridge: Cambridge University Press, 1922 (1903).
The Religion of Ancient Greece, London: Archibald Constable & Co. Ltd., 1905.
Themis, A Study of the Social Origins of Greek Religion, Cambridge: Cambridge University Press, 1912.

E. O. James, *The Cult of the Mother-Goddess: An Archaeological and Documentary Study*, New York: Frederick A. Praeger, Inc., 1959.

C. G. Jung and C. Kerenyi, *Essays on a Science of Mythology*, translated by R. F. C. Hull, New York: Pantheon Books, 1949.

C. Kerenyi, *Zeus and Hera*, translated by Christopher Holme, Princeton: Princeton University Press (Bollingen Series 65-5), 1975.

Lady-Unique-Inclination-of-the-Night, periodical journal, P.O. Box 803, New Brunswick, New Jersey 08903.

New Larousse Encyclopedia of Mythology, 1968 Edition, London and New York: The Hamlyn Publishing Group Ltd., 1976.

Friedrich Matz, *The Art of Crete and Early Greece*, New York: Crown Publishers Inc., 1962.

George E. Mylonas, *The Hymn to Demeter and Her Sanctuary at Eleusis*, St. Louis: Washington University Language and Literature Series, No. 13, 1942.

Erich Neumann, *The Great Mother: An Analysis of the Archetype*, translated by Ralph Manheim, Princeton: Princeton University Press (Bollingen Series 47), 1963 (1955).

Martin P. Nilsson, *Greek Popular Religion*, New York: Columbia University Press, 1947 (1940).
A History of Greek Religion, Oxford: Oxford University Press, 1949 (1925).
The Minoan-Mycenaean Religion, New York: Biblo and Tannen, 1971 (1950).

Adrienne Rich, *Of Woman Born*, New York: W. W. Norton & Co., 1976.

Sandra Roos, "Roots of Feminine Consciousness in Prehistoric Art," unpublished article manuscript, 1977.

H. J. Rose, *A Handbook of Greek Mythology*, New York: E. P. Dutton & Co., Inc., 1950 (1928).

Anne Kent Rush, *Moon, Moon,* Berkeley and New York: Moon Books/Random House, 1976.

Carolee Schneemann, *HOMERUNMUSE, A Lecture on the Feminist Goddess Roots of Art*, Schneemann Books, 114 West 29th Street, N.Y., N.Y. 10001.

Philip E. Slater, *The Glory of Hera*, Boston: Beacon Press, 1968.

Merlin Stone, *When God Was A Woman*, New York: The Dial Press, 1976.

George Thomson, *The Prehistoric Aegean*, New York: The Citadel Press, 1965 (1949).

R. F. Willetts, *Cretan Cults and Festivals*, London:
Routledge and Kegan Paul, 1962.

WomanSpirit, quarterly journal, P.O. Box 263,
Wolf Creek, Oregon 97497.

Gunther Zuntz, *Persephone: Three Essays on
Religion and Thought in Magna Graecia*,
Oxford: Oxford University Press, 1971.

Charlene Spretnak is a writer and an editor. Her fiction, essays, and reviews have appeared in various periodicals. She lives in Berkeley with her daughter.

Edidt Geever began her career in Vienna as a graphic designer. Her interest in illustration and book design formulated through work in Switzerland and Germany. Presently her studio is in Northern California.